Series Editor - Julia...

How to Handle Money

A Short Guide to Financial Accountability

CHRIS WRIGHT
Foreword by Femi B. Adeleye

THE DIDASKO FILES

This developing series takes its name from the New Testament Greek verb *didasko*, meaning 'I teach'. We trust it will serve the world's Church by helping Christians to grow in their faith.

The idea for the Didasko project came from the International Fellowship of Evangelical Students (IFES), now in more than 150 countries, working to proclaim Christ in the world's universities. www.ifesworld.org. To extend its reach, the series was transferred to The Lausanne Movement, in which IFES plays an active role. www.lausanne.org

www.didaskofiles.com

How to Handle Money: A Small Guide to Financial Accountability
© 2013 The Lausanne Movement

Hendrickson Publishers Marketing, LLC
P. O. Box 3473
Peabody, Massachusetts 01961-3473
www.hendrickson.com

ISBN 978-1-61970-025-3

Published in this format by arrangement with Didasko Publishing, a non-profit entity working on behalf of The Lausanne Movement.

This document may be reproduced in whole or in part, without permission, for personal or ministry use only. The text should remain unchanged and should include: © 2013 The Lausanne Movement.

For publishing rights in translation for all titles in this series, go to www.didaskofiles.com

All royalties from this series will be used for publishing endeavours relating to The Lausanne Movement.

Printed in China

First Hendrickson Edition Printing — January 2013

Scriptures taken from the Holy Bible, New International Version®, NIV®. Copyright © 1973, 1978, 1984, 2011 by Biblica, Inc.™ Used by permission of Zondervan. All rights reserved worldwide. www.zondervan.com The "NIV" and "New International Version" are trademarks registered in the United States Patent and Trademark Office by Biblica, Inc.™ (Italics in quoted Scriptures are author's emphasis.)

How to Handle Money

A Short Guide to Financial Accountability

EDITOR'S NOTE

Church leaders and mission leaders may like to be aware of John Stott's *The Grace of Giving*, also in this series. Chris Wright has provided the Foreword. That booklet and this are companions.

The Grace of Giving is for all church members and mission supporters, and this publication is for those who are charged with the responsibility of handling the money received. John Stott helps Christians to consider personally, before God, in an unhurried way, both how much to give and where to focus their giving. He shows how all Christian giving (whether to a church, to evangelistic mission, to capital funds such as building projects, or to development work) is linked directly to the doctrine of the Holy Trinity. We are pleased to commend it.

Julia Cameron
Series Editor

CONTENTS

Foreword

Author's Preface

1. Financial *support for the poor* is integral to biblical mission

2. Financial *administration* is a stewardship of grace and obedience

3. Financial *appeals* require advance planning

4. Financial *temptations* call for 'safety in numbers'

5. Financial *accountability* demands transparency before God and man

6. Financial *trustworthiness* is an apostolic honour to Christ

FOREWORD

The six principles Chris Wright highlights to us from the Apostle Paul are so important that they are non-negotiable.

Christians too often respond to the subject of financial resources inadequately, either by regarding it as primarily secular, having little bearing on spiritual matters, or by remaining indifferent to it. To the Church's shame, there are others who use it to manipulate, either to gain more funding, or to offer false promises, as with proponents of the 'prosperity gospel'.

Almost every private space, and the entire public arena, is now market-driven. In the privacy of our homes, and even in the sacred place of public worship, we are under pressure to become consumers. This increases temptation to acquire more of what we don't really need and diminishes our discernment of God's call on us, with regards to the needs of others.

We shall all be shaped by either the values society imposes on us or by the biblical principles so clearly articulated here. Many will be surprised by Chris's assertion that, on the plain level of number of verses, Paul 'gives more text space to writing about issues related to financial affairs of churches than he does to writing about justification by faith'. The spiritual nature of this subject is clear, and the Apostle Paul's theology of money, as God-centred and mission-centred, deserves keen attention. A safety net of accountability is critical for those in positions of responsibility, to whom resources have been entrusted.

So we need to consider Paul's teaching closely. I commend the words of Chris Wright as he challenges us, through this *Didasko File*, to be more deliberate in engaging with this subject, as part of a God-focused, Christ-centred, and Spirit-led life.

Femi B. Adeleye
International Fellowship of Evangelical Students

AUTHOR'S PREFACE

To find out what the New Testament teaches about financial accountability in the church, and by extension in all Christian ministry endeavours, let's look at the practice of the Apostle Paul.

There was to be a collection of money from churches in the Roman provinces of Macedonia and Achaia (present-day Greece) to alleviate poverty of other Christians. The money was to be taken to the believers in Jerusalem, where there was evidently a great deal of poverty, and the Apostle Paul oversaw the arrangements. For Paul it was important for one part of the Christian church to help another part in this way.

Paul's references to this collection of money (what he taught about it and the safeguards he put in place) are instructive for us. They show Paul's strong sense of accountability, transparency, and integrity. His example and his teaching apply just as much now, to the financial affairs of churches, missions, and special projects, as they did then.

it was important for one part of the church to help another part

Paul makes use of the collection as an occasion for teaching. He gives more textual space in his letters to writing about it than he does to writing about justification by faith. That probably surprises us. To state it does not belittle Paul's doctrine of justification or any of his great doctrinal teaching.

We will look at three major passages and a few shorter ones. The major passages are 1 Corinthians 16, where Paul refers to this collection; 2 Corinthians 8–9, where he devotes space to general principles of giving; and Romans 15. (For background: Macedonia is in the northern part of Greece, and the Corinthians, to whom Paul is writing, were in the southern part of Greece, so you will see a kind of north/south rivalry going on.) We see six clear principles at work.

Chris Wright
London

1

Financial *support for the poor* is integral to biblical mission

Paul sees no dichotomy between his evangelistic church-planting mission and his efforts to bring about the relief of poverty among the believers in Jerusalem. Financial support for the poor is a biblical mandate. For Paul this is all part of his task, his mission, and his calling.

Let us step sideways for a moment, to Galatians 2. Here we again see the mandate for the poor. It is not the central focus of Paul's teaching, yet its place in Paul's argument lends particular weight to it. Here Paul is defending three things. He defends (1) his apostolic authority, (2) the content and nature of his apostolic gospel, and (3) the rightness of preaching the gospel to the Gentile Christians, the *Galati*, a branch of the great nations of the Celts that had migrated into southern Turkey. Paul had preached the gospel to them, and they had become believers. Then Paul faced the great theological controversy with the Jewish believers as to how these non-Jewish people could be accepted into the covenant and into the people of God. Some of the Jewish believers had come to Galatia and troubled the Galatian churches, trying to insist that they must become circumcised and observe the Mosaic Law.

it is important for believers to grasp matters clearly

Paul writes the Epistle to the Galatians against that background, to defend the fact that his gospel had been accepted as fully authentic by the apostles in Jerusalem. The New Testament church is very young, and it is important for believers to grasp matters clearly. Paul's deep passion for truth and clarity is what lies behind Galatians 2. He declares that he had received his teaching from the Lord but had submitted it to the apostles in Jerusalem, and they had accepted that it was authentic and true. He states: 'James,

HOW TO HANDLE MONEY

Peter, and John, those reputed to be pillars, gave me and Barnabas the right hand of *koinonia*—the right hand of fellowship—when they recognized the grace given to me. They agreed that we should go to the Gentiles, and they to the Jews. All they asked was that we should continue to remember the poor, the very thing I was eager to do' (Galatians 2:9–10).

The 'right hand of fellowship' is not simply a token of friendship. The word *koinonia* means much more. It is a sharing *in* and a sharing *of* what God has given to us, and that affects the financial dimension as well as the spiritual dimension of our corporate life. So in Acts chapters 2 and 4 we read about the *koinonia* of the early church in Jerusalem. Certainly, it was a spiritual *koinonia*. Believers shared in the apostles' teaching, in the breaking of bread, and in prayers. But it was also a financial *koinonia*; they shared with one another to relieve poverty. It is clear from what Paul says in Galatians 2 that this spirit of the church in Jerusalem was still operating; the Jerusalem church still cared about the poor in their midst. They saw it as an essential part of gospel *koinonia*. So if Paul the apostle was going to be a partner with them and share in their understanding of the gospel, then he too must be committed to remembering the poor as part of his gospel credentials. It was, he says, the very thing he was eager to do anyway. So we learn that active financial concern for the poor is how the Jerusalem church operated, and it was part of Paul's commitment.

> *they shared with one another to relieve poverty*

At the end of Paul's letter to the church in Rome (Romans 15), Paul writes about his lifelong commitment to church planting and evangelistic ministry. Earlier in the chapter he explained how God had given him grace 'to be a minister of Christ Jesus to the Gentiles with the priestly duty of proclaiming the gospel of God,' so that the Gentiles were becoming an offering to God (vv 15–16). That is his ministry, and that is what he believes he is called to do. He has now done it all around the eastern Mediterranean basin, from Jerusalem to Illyricum (now modern Albania). He continues: 'I have fully proclaimed the gospel of Christ. It has always been my ambition to preach the gospel where Christ was not known, so that I would not be building on someone else's foundation. . . . But now . . . there is no more place for me to work in these regions' (vv 19–20, 23).

CHRIS WRIGHT

So now Paul is planning a bold missionary project that will take him to the western half of the Mediterranean, toward Spain. That is his great evangelistic vision, and he is looking forward to visiting the Christians in Rome on the way. But *at the moment*, says Paul, my priority is to go to Jerusalem in the service of the saints there. 'For Macedonia and Achaia were pleased to make a contribution for the poor among the saints in Jerusalem. They were pleased to do it, and indeed they owe it to them. For if the Gentiles have shared in the Jews' spiritual blessings, they owe it to the Jews to share with them their material blessings. So after I have completed this task and have made sure that they have received this fruit, I will go to Spain and visit you on the way. I know that when I come to you, I will come in the full measure of the blessing of Christ' (vv 26–29).

Look carefully at what he says a bit later: 'Pray that I may be rescued from the unbelievers in Judea and that my service in Jerusalem may be acceptable to the saints there, so that by God's will I may come to you with joy and together with you be refreshed' (vv 31–32).

Paul in effect puts his evangelistic strategy on hold, to carry out his *relief of poverty strategy*. It is interesting that at this point Paul does not say, 'I've got to go on to evangelize Spain, so I'll dump the responsibility for this financial gift onto somebody else; they can take it to Jerusalem. My job is to preach the gospel, not to relieve the poor.' Paul sees no conflict in making his priority at this point his service to the saints through the relief of poverty. So first he will take the collected money to the people in Jerusalem. Not only does he see it as a personal priority; he asks for prayer for it. He asks for prayer just as later he would ask for prayer when he was in prison (when he asked people to pray for courage to preach the gospel). Just as he called on believers to pray for him in his evangelistic ministry, here he asks the Roman Christians to pray for him in his financial ministry to the saints in Jerusalem.

Paul puts his evangelistic strategy on hold

He does not perceive this task as an unavoidable interruption in his evangelistic career. To complete this work of poverty-relief will be to fulfil a Christ-centred calling; as much so as when he was completing his evangelistic mandate. When he has done this, he says, 'I will come to you in the

HOW TO HANDLE MONEY

full measure of Christ'. What a rich phrase, carrying with it a deep sense of fulfilling Christ's calling.

Paul sees no dichotomy between these two dimensions of ministry. Indeed, as one writer has said, 'We do not know if Paul achieved this mission [his evangelistic plans to go to Spain], but we do know that he delivered the collection [to relieve the poor in Jerusalem]. *The collection was so vital that its delivery was at that moment a more urgent matter for Paul than his desire to evangelize and plant churches on the missionary frontier'.*[1]

In 1 Timothy 6 Paul instructs Timothy to pass this teaching on to the church. The responsibility for generous giving by those who have the means is core to our Christian commitment and part of our response to the gospel. Paul says, 'Command those who are rich in this present world not to be arrogant nor to put their hope in wealth, which is so uncertain, but to put their hope in God, who richly provides us with everything for our enjoyment. Command them [note this second use of 'command'] to do good, to be rich in good deeds, and to be generous and willing to share' (1 Timothy 6:17–18).

The English conceals the fact that the Greek word is *koinonikos* ['willing to share']. They are to share their fellowship by their financial generosity, and in this way they will lay up treasure for themselves as a firm foundation for the coming age, echoing the teaching of Jesus.

Generosity is a Christian duty

Generosity is a Christian duty, says Paul, something that pastors can command. He is probably echoing Deuteronomy 15, where God says to the Israelites (vv 10–11, 14–15), 'Give generously to him [the poor person] and do so without a grudging heart; then because of this the LORD your God will bless you. . . . There will always be poor people in the land [or in the world]. Therefore I command you to be openhanded toward your brothers. . . . Give to him [that is, the poor person] as the LORD your God has blessed you. Remember that you were slaves in Egypt and the LORD your God redeemed you. That is why I give you this command today'.

---

[1]. Jason Hood, 'Theology in Action: Paul and Christian Social Care', in *Transforming the World: The Gospel and Social Responsibility*, ed. Jamie A. Grant and Dewi A. Hughes (Nottingham: IVP Apollos, 2009), pp 129–46. Quotation taken from p 134; italics original.

CHRIS WRIGHT

Summary Principle 1: Paul saw generous financial support for the poor and careful administration of that gift as integral to biblical mission, gospel mission. It was part of what he was called to do, as well as the more obviously evangelistic tasks of preaching and planting churches.

HOW TO HANDLE MONEY

2

Financial *administration* is a stewardship of grace and obedience

When we handle money given by God's people, we are handling (1) the fruit of God's grace and (2) practical proof of human obedience to the gospel. Money that has been given as an offering to God is not just 'stuff'. It is not just coins and notes or covenants or ledgers or entries in a journal. When we handle money that has been given by God's people, we are involved in a deeply spiritual matter. God's people give in response to God's kindness. As we handle that money we are entrusted with something; we are stewards of the fruit of grace in their lives and stewards of the proof of obedience.

This understanding of our stewardship comes from what Paul says at the beginning of chapter 8 and the end of chapter 9 of 1 Corinthians. Notice how frequently the word 'grace' occurs in these familiar words.

> Now, brothers, we want you to know about the *grace* that God has given the Macedonian churches. Out of the most severe trial, their overflowing joy and their extreme poverty welled up in rich generosity. For I testify that they gave as much as they were able, and even beyond their ability. Entirely on their own, they urgently pleaded with us for the privilege of sharing in this service to the saints. And they did not do as we expected, but they gave themselves first to the Lord and then to us in keeping with God's will. So we urged Titus, since he had earlier made a beginning, to bring also to completion this act of *grace* on your part. But just as you excel in everything—in faith, in speech, in knowledge, in complete earnestness and in your love for us—see that you also excel in this *grace* of giving. (2 Corinthians 8:1–7)

Three times Paul uses the word 'grace' about the Macedonian believers, and a couple of verses later he talks about 'the *grace* of our Lord Jesus Christ.' Note that the word *koinonia* is in there again. This desire to give was a mark of their *koinonia*, their fellowship.

This gift of the Macedonians, Paul writes, was a response to the Lord ('they gave themselves first to the Lord'). Moreover, it was something that they wanted to do. They did not have to be asked to give; they asked for the privilege of giving. Because of the grace of God in them, they responded in an act of grace to others. This is reciprocal grace, or grace being expressed in action.

Paul sends Titus to oversee and administer the collection. It is as if Paul was saying (and I think this is slightly the flavour of his wording), 'Because this is such an important evidence of the grace of God and of the fruit of the gospel in the lives of these believers, I am sending my most trusted senior person to handle this responsibility'. He did not send a junior clerk or some young functionary who might be haphazard in dealing with it all. Paul says, in effect, 'It is a serious matter, so we urged Titus—an apostolic delegate in the church—to go and make sure that it was properly handled and treated with the seriousness it deserves'.

This display of generosity was not just an act of grace, but also an act of obedience. 'This service that you perform is not only supplying the needs of God's people but is also overflowing in many expressions of thanks to God. Because of the service by which you [that is, you Gentiles] have proved yourselves, men will praise God for the obedience that accompanies your confession of the gospel of Christ, and for your generosity in sharing with them [*koinonia* again] and with everyone else. And in their prayers for you their hearts will go out to you because of the surpassing grace God has given you' (2 Corinthians 9:12–15).

And, Paul adds, 'Thanks be to God for *his* indescribable gift!' which of course is the Lord Jesus Christ.

According to Paul giving, sharing, and generosity are not just grace; they are also proof of obedience. Why was that important? Precisely because these were Gentiles. The Jewish believers in Jerusalem were still uncertain whether or not these Gentiles, who had never been circumcised and were not keeping the Law, were really part of the family. Did they really belong to the covenant people of God? Paul responds, 'The fact that you Gentiles have given an offering to meet the needs of Jewish believers is a proof of the fellowship that we have in Christ. Your obedience to the gospel is a

HOW TO HANDLE MONEY

demonstration that though you have been so despised by the Jews historically, you are now at one with them; that there is no difference, there is no Jew or Gentile, male or female, slave or free'. Let's not miss the profound significance here. This gift was a proof of obedience to the core meaning of the gospel.

Let's not miss the profound significance here

Summary Principle 2: Handling a gift offered by God's people is a sacred trust. Administering it is a stewardship of the grace of God and of the obedience of God's people to the gospel. Paul's concern for accountability, integrity, and transparency was not just to satisfy the Roman governors or other officials. It arose because he was dealing with something coming from God: the grace of God and obedience to the gospel.

3
Financial *appeals* require advance planning

Look how thoroughly Paul prepares the way for the gift. In 1 Corinthians he has been answering a lot of questions from the church, and he comes back to something that he has told them about before, but wants to raise again. He wants them to be ready and prepared. 'Now about the collection for God's people: Do what I told the Galatian churches to do. On the first day of every week, each one of you should set aside a sum of money in keeping with his income, saving it up, so that when I come no collections will have to be made. Then, when I arrive, I will give letters of introduction to the men you approve and send them with your gift to Jerusalem' (1 Corinthians 16:1–3).

In 2 Corinthians 9:1–5 Paul shows the same concern for preparedness. 'There is no need for me to write to you about this service to the saints. For I know your eagerness to help, and I have been boasting about it to the Macedonians, telling them that since last year you in Achaia were ready to give [again catch the note of north/south rivalry]; and your enthusiasm has stirred most of them to action. But I am sending the brothers [that is, I am sending some people in advance] in order that our boasting about you in this matter should not prove hollow, but that you may be ready, as I said you would be. For if any Macedonians come with me and find you unprepared, we ... would be ashamed of having been so confident. So I thought it necessary to urge the brothers to visit you in advance and finish the arrangements for the generous gift you had promised. Then it will be ready as a generous gift, not as one grudgingly given' (that is, pulled together at the last minute).

> *Paul wants giving to be thought about, prayed about, and prepared for*

HOW TO HANDLE MONEY

Can you see what Paul is doing here? He does not want this collection to become debased into an emotional appeal in which everybody is urged to put their hands in their pockets, and the music goes on until everybody has dug deeper, and then the offering buckets are sent around again. No, Paul is purposely avoiding that type of emotional manipulation. He does not want there to be any kind of 'on-the-spot' pressure for a gift that has not been carefully thought through. Paul wants his collection and the giving by the church to be something that has been thought about, prayed about, and prepared for. It should be systematic (we should plan what we will give); it should be regular (week by week setting money aside); it should be proportionate (according to income, with those who have more giving more); the means of collecting should be transparent (the brothers will come and they will oversee it); and the total collected should be public (announced and recorded). All of this preparation and supervision is built into Paul's careful planning.

> *Paul wants this offering to be planned well in advance*

Accountability is not just an afterthought; it is not something you try to sort out after the event—'All this money has come in, how wonderful! Now we'd better decide what we do with it, who is going to count it, who is going to bank it, and who will keep accounts'. Accountability is not just a matter of reacting when problems arise. It should be planned; it should be built in from the very start. Paul says, 'Look, here is what we are planning. This is what we're asking *you* to do, and this is what *we* will then do when you have done what we ask'. The whole procedure is a matter of shared responsibility. Paul does not want their giving to be mere opportunism: 'Paul's come to town again; let's have a quick collection and give him a love gift'. No, Paul wants this offering to be carefully thought through and planned well in advance, so that nobody will be taken by surprise and nobody can be accused of emotional manipulation. That is an important way by which he builds accountability into his financial relationship with the church.

Notice that Paul is concerned, also, about loss of face. The world of ancient Greece and Rome is a relational economy, so he conducts this offering relationally. He says, 'Some of our brothers will be coming to you, and I will be coming later as well, and we don't want any embarrassment. I don't want you to lose face; I don't want you to be ashamed, and I don't want them to be gloating. So let's do this properly, and let's plan it and have it all out on the table clear and open, so that everybody is satisfied'.

Summary Principle 3: Proper planning of financial appeals is important, and safeguards should be set up before the event.

HOW TO HANDLE MONEY

4

Financial *temptations* call for 'safety in numbers'

Wherever there is money, there is temptation. This is just as true for Christians as anybody else, so it is wise to protect ourselves from temptation by having more than one person involved in handling the money. This way of working was true of Paul's ministry in general. He was a great individual minister, preacher, gospel letter writer, and everything else. But generally he did not operate alone. He was the leader, but he worked with teams that included people such as Silas, Barnabas, Timothy, and Titus. Indeed, when Paul did find himself completely alone, he was distressed about it. In 2 Timothy 4:16 there are heartrending words when everyone has deserted him; this was terrible for him. He wanted to be in a team; he wanted to belong with others.

Great emphasis is laid on the plurality of people involved in handling money. Knowing exactly who was involved becomes quite complicated, but evidently there were several people. In 1 Corinthians 16:3-4 Paul says, 'I will give letters of introduction to the men you approve'—in other words, those whom the Christians in Corinth trusted. Then offering to do the task himself, he writes, 'If it seems advisable for me to go also, they will accompany me.' So he would not take charge of the money by himself, but would involve others.

It is also difficult to know how many are involved in 2 Corinthians 8:16-24, but we can identify some. 'I thank God, who put into the heart of Titus the same concern I have for you. For Titus not only welcomed our appeal, but he is coming to you with much enthusiasm and on his own initiative. And we are sending along with him the brother who is praised by all the churches for his service to the gospel [this was a trusted Christian leader]. What is more, he was chosen by the churches to accompany us'. So he was someone elected or chosen and appointed to exercise this financial responsibility. In addition to this, 'We are sending with them our brother [Paul does not name him] who has often proved to us in many ways that he is zealous, and now even more so because of his great confidence in you' (v 22).

So the point is, certainly more than one person was involved, and they were all trusted people. They were accepted and known by everybody. There was no anonymity. Christian accountability is a matter of trust between fellow believers, but Paul shows us the wisdom of building in safeguards of plurality, because even believers are still sinners and few things are more tempting than money. Paul is well aware that even trusted brothers can go astray. Sadly, we read about a few of them at the end of his letters when he writes that some who preferred the world and the world's ways have gone off and left him (e.g., 2 Timothy 4:10). Paul knew that even the best people need the protection of relational accountability to one another.

So then, Paul insists on plurality in the handling of money. It is a very wise principle to adopt in any church or Christian endeavour. In many UK churches, certainly in my own church at All Souls, gift money is never counted by only one person. When the offering is brought to the vestry, there are always at least two and sometimes three or four people in the room. The door is then closed, and they count the offering together. They are a check on one another. Now of course, we all trust one another; nobody expects that anybody is going to be doing anything wrong, but there is need for openness and verifiability in handling money. We need to be above suspicion.

even trusted brothers can go astray

Many organizations, including my own, will not allow bank cheques to be signed by only one person; there must always be two signatories to manage the bank account and the finances. That is another wise practice.

How do we make that work in a cultural setting where it is unthinkable to question the honour and authority of the senior leader—least of all by calling him to account over money? That would be to break the relationship and cause loss of face. So how should we ensure proper accountability? Perhaps here the leaders themselves should take the initiative. They could

HOW TO HANDLE MONEY

choose to say, 'Please, will you join me as we do this? I request that other people should be involved with me as we arrange our financial affairs, or as we handle these funds, or as we set up this Trust. I want other people alongside myself to see how the money is handled and how the decisions are made. I want them to be completely satisfied that all is being done transparently and honourably'. In that way the person at the top is able to lead from the top and to set the example, just as the Apostle Paul did. Paul could easily have said, 'I'm an apostle. Trust me. I'll do this myself'. But he did not. He insisted *from the top* that there should be others alongside him to ensure it was all done honestly. If a leader does this *voluntarily*, he is not saying to those under him, 'I think you don't trust me'. Rather he is saying, 'I know you trust me. And because you trust me, I want to make sure that your trust is never betrayed. I want to be completely transparent, and therefore I choose to share my accountability with other trusted Christian friends and brothers'.

Summary Principle 4: To introduce higher standards of accountability, we must lead by example. Accountability is something we as leaders should choose to have, for our own good and for the protection of the Lord's name, not something that is forced upon us.

5

Financial *accountability* demands transparency before God and man

I love the fact that when Paul has finished talking about all the people he is bringing into the team to deliver the money to Jerusalem, he explains why he is handling it in this plural way.

'We want to avoid any criticism of the way we administer this liberal gift. For we are taking pains to do what is right, not only in the eyes of the Lord, but also in the eyes of men' (2 Corinthians 8:20–21).

These verses express a principle that is transcultural. That is, they provide a biblical model for us, whatever our culture or background. They are challenging and very significant. I think they should be hung up on the wall of any room where a Christian organization does its financial business.

The arrangements Paul put in place were not only very careful but also probably quite costly. It would cost a lot more for five or six men to travel from Greece to Jerusalem than for Paul to go there by himself; travel was not cheap in those days. So the arrangements Paul was building up around this gift could have aroused resistance. Church members could have said, 'Why send so many people? You are going to waste some of the gift on their expenses' (just as we complain about the cost of auditing our accounts). But Paul says, 'It's worth that cost because I don't want any criticism; I want to be completely transparent before God and people, so that nothing we do can be open to criticism'.

Paul was operating within a culture that had similarities to some non-Western cultures today. The Greek and Roman cultures were very top-down, very hierarchical. The Roman system was patron-client oriented. The men at the top were patrons: they were bankers or politicians; they were wealthy, and people would come to their homes every day wanting favours. Being

HOW TO HANDLE MONEY

in with the top man was crucially important; that is how Roman politics worked. It was a very relational economy in that sense.

So Paul is acting counterculturally in what he does with this gift. He could have said, 'I'm the boss; I'm your patron; I'm the apostle. Give me the money and a single armed guard, and I'll take it to Jerusalem. Just trust me'. Instead he says, 'No, I want this to be completely transparent, so I must have others with me to make sure all is done properly and above criticism'.

> *He could have said, 'I'll take it to Jerusalem. Just trust me.'*

I would love 2 Corinthians 8:21 to become a motto for each of us as Christ's followers; something that we take to heart: 'We are taking pains to do what is right, not only in the eyes of the Lord, but also in the eyes of men'. Let us make this principle a motto for each of us and for all our mission organizations. What a difference it could make, and how it could help to prevent some of the tragic scandals of fraud and theft and mismanagement within Christian organizations.

Summary Principle 5: The vertical and the horizontal are both needed. Paul says, 'We should be able to trust one another in the Lord, but we want to do what is beyond criticism in the eyes of the watching world as well'.

CHRIS WRIGHT

6

Financial *trustworthiness* is an apostolic honour to Christ

Let's look at upward and downward accountability. We tend to think that we are *upwardly* accountable to bodies such as boards and funding foundations and donors and the government and legal authorities, and *downwardly* accountable to our beneficiaries, that is, to those who actually receive from our ministry, those whom we are serving. However, the direction of our accountability is the reverse. Our *upward* accountability is to those who occupy the position Jesus was referring to when he said, 'Inasmuch as you do it to the least of these my brethren, you do it for me' (see Matthew 25:40). Those our ministry is serving are actually Jesus to us. So our accountability to them is really our accountability to him—which is 'upward'. When we serve others in our ministry, we are serving Christ. We are honouring him in serving them.

Paul says in several passages that discharging this financial responsibility in a trustworthy manner is an honour to Christ, not just a matter of transparency before men. It was important to do the job with honesty and integrity. But even more, it was important to do it for the honour and glory of Christ. Look first at 2 Corinthians 8:18–19. Who were these people who were administering the gift? Paul says, 'We are sending along with him [Titus] the brother who is praised by all the churches for his service to the gospel. What is more, he was chosen by the churches'. Titus was an honoured person whose life was already seen to be honouring to the Lord and honouring to the gospel, and therefore Paul and the Corinthians could trust him with their money. And the way he handles the money will also be honouring to the Lord and to the church. Honest finances are honouring to Christ (with the obvious implication that dishonesty dishonours Christ).

HOW TO HANDLE MONEY

The point is even more explicit in verses 23 and 24. 'As for Titus, he is my partner and fellow worker among you; as for our brothers, they are representatives of the churches *and an honour to Christ*. Therefore show these men the proof of your love and the reason for our pride in you, so that the churches can see it'. The word 'representatives', used there, is actually *apostoloi*, apostles. It is used in the weaker sense that occurs several times in the New Testament to refer to others beyond the twelve apostolic pillars of the church (the twelve disciples, minus Judas Iscariot and plus Matthias in the Book of Acts, and then the Apostle Paul). In this slightly looser sense, the word *apostolos* meant someone who was an emissary or a trusted delegate of the churches. There seem to have been a number of these apostolic delegates—Titus, Timothy, and others who are mentioned in 3 John and elsewhere. So Paul says, these *apostoloi*, these chosen delegates of the churches who are being entrusted with the responsibility of handling finances within the churches, especially this large financial gift to Jerusalem, are an honour to Christ.

What a commendation! What a way to speak of an accountant or treasurer! These people are entrusted with money. And by being faithful in that trust, they are not only an honour to Christ, but also they should have church approval (v 24): 'Show these men the proof of your love', because we want them to be seen by all the churches.

What a way to speak of an accountant or treasurer!

Look at how Paul speaks about Epaphroditus in Philippians 2:25–30. He says, 'I think it is necessary to send back to you Epaphroditus, my brother, fellow worker and fellow soldier, who is also your messenger'. Again the word is *apostolos*, your apostle. Epaphroditus was not an apostle in the sense that Paul was, but he was the emissary, the representative, the trusted messenger of the church, and hence apostolic. Paul continues, 'whom you sent to take care of my needs. For he longs for all of you and is distressed because you heard he was ill. Indeed he was ill, and almost died. But God had mercy on him, and not on him only but also on me, to spare me sorrow upon sorrow. Therefore I am all the more eager to send him [back]. . . . Welcome him in the Lord with great joy, and honor men like him, because he almost died for the work of Christ, risking his life to make up for the help you could not

CHRIS WRIGHT

give me'. What Paul is describing is Epaphroditus's handling of the financial and material gift that the Philippian church had made to Paul when Paul was in need. And Paul says in effect, 'That service of Epaphroditus was a work of the gospel; that was a work born out of love for Christ and for his church. Epaphroditus nearly died doing what he did and, therefore,' Paul says, 'honour him. What he is doing, he is doing for Christ's sake'.

In Philippians 4:14–19 we find another reference to the same thing, the gift that was sent to Paul through Epaphroditus. Verse 18 reads, 'I have received full payment and even more; I am amply supplied, now that I have received from Epaphroditus the gifts you sent. They are a fragrant offering, an acceptable sacrifice, pleasing to God'. Epaphroditus's role then, says Paul, was an apostolic honour: serving God and serving Christ by serving the servants of God. In serving the servants of God, people like Epaphroditus are deserving of honour and respect, because they are an honour to Christ himself.

To administer financial affairs with trustworthiness, with transparency, with honesty as did Epaphroditus and others in the New Testament, is a Christ-honouring thing to do: we do it for him.

When I was the principal of All Nations Christian College near London, there was a time when issues arose that affected me personally. The chairman of the college Board of Directors was a very wise, godly brother whom I greatly respected. I was required to give account of some aspects of how I was running things and reasons for decisions that had been made. That was not easy; it is not comfortable to have people poking into everything that is going on. That is true even if you have nothing troubling your conscience. I knew that in relation to the college I had done nothing wrong, but still I had to accept the questioning. At one point, the chairman of the Council said, 'Chris, accountability is not a burden; it's a *gift*. It's a gift that we give you. We hold you accountable, and that is for your good; it's for your protection. It's not something we are imposing upon you. It's something we are *giving* to you because we love you, because you are a brother in Christ, and we want to affirm your integrity by expecting proper accountability'. I

> *To administer financial affairs with transparency is Christ-honouring*

HOW TO HANDLE MONEY

thought that was a very helpful, positive way for me to look at the demanding challenge of accountability. I learned to see it, not as a threat or an insult or 'beneath my dignity to be questioned', but as something that was honouring to me and also, of course, to God.

we want to affirm your integrity by expecting accountability

Summary Principle 6: In 1 Samuel 2:30 God said through a prophet to Eli, 'Those who honor me I will honor'. If we want the Lord's honour, we need to be honourable in the way we handle money and in the way we hold ourselves accountable; we need to be transparent men and women of integrity in everything. Let us make Paul and his teaching on this matter a powerful and authoritative model for ourselves.

CHRIS WRIGHT

May we all pray for God to grant us the courage to live and work with complete integrity, and may we honour one another by expecting—and giving—accountability to one another and to the Lord.

HOW TO HANDLE MONEY

QUESTIONS FOR REFLECTION

What steps can you take to help your church sustain practical concern for the poor in (1) your locality? (2) your nation? (3) the world?

Are there more safeguards your church or ministry should put in place to protect those who handle money?

Appeal letters should state needs openly and not exaggerate past triumphs or future possibilities. Long-term spiritual ministry does not always see exciting results. If your church members or your donors respond only to exciting stories, how can you help them grasp this?

Treasurers and Finance Committee members, like all spiritual leaders, must be men and women of Christian character. In addition they need relevant gifting and experience. Does your church or ministry have good structures in place (1) for appointing these officers? (2) for their reporting to (a) the leadership? (b) the membership?

CHRIS WRIGHT

THE DIDASKO FILES

An Authentic Servant: The Marks of a Spiritual Leader by Ajith Fernando

John Stott: Pastor, Leader and Friend (several contributors)

Light, Salt and the World of Business: Good Practice Can Change Nations by Fred Catherwood

More Precious than Gold: Read the Bible in One or Two Years (McCheyne Bible Reading Plan)

The Glory of the Cross: The Great Crescendo of the Gospel by James Philip

The Grace of Giving: Ten Principles of Christian Giving by John Stott

The Lausanne Covenant: The Complete Text with Study Guide

The Cape Town Commitment: A Confession of Faith and a Call to Action

How to Handle Money: A Short Guide to Financial Accountability by Chris Wright

Further titles in preparation

The Didasko Files (English language edition) are published in partnership with Hendrickson Publishers and may be sourced through most internet retailers. Some titles are available in formats for Visually Impaired People.

www.didaskofiles.com
www.hendrickson.com